L POEMS

MAC GABBERT

MINML POEMS

MAG GABBERT

Cooper
Dillon

Acknowledgments:
mutiny!: "pfflustrd," "pleaseant," "ceyecle," "joak,"
"rabbid"; *The Freshwater Review:* "studebt,"
"gnormal"; *The Hopkins Review:* "m o c n," "l c s s,"
"anammal," "woolf," "whail"

Portions of "When Believing is Seeing" appeared
in *White Stag* and *The Nervous Breakdown*

Cooper Dillon Books
San Diego, California
CooperDillon.com

Cover Image: "Australia" by Olga Gál
                    www.artolgagal.com
Book Design: Adam Deutsch
ISBN:978-1-943899-11-1

Table of Contents

Here is my honey-machine,
It will work without thinking

—Sylvia Plath, "Stings"

pleaseant

lauaugh

plaiffle

anammal

woolf

whail

rabbid

phemmale

phallucy

studebt

whyyyfe

womn

blead

ceyecle

lcss

m o c n

wwAvve

implocean

spasgm

springle

whimdow

starlte

clowd

festume

pfigment

ghaunted

gnormal

joak

faer

faeairy

ghoary

poultrygeist

pfiggy

spounffle

crumbple

garbbage

pfflustrd

When Believing is Seeing

It's a chilly evening in late April, and I am standing in the lobby outside a small private parlor at The Adolphus Hotel in downtown Dallas. Like the one hundred and fifty or so people planted anxiously in front of and behind me in line, I have come here to see Chip Coffey, a world-renowned psychic medium who's been featured on countless television and radio programs, including A&E's TV series *Paranormal State*, the spin-off series *Psychic Kids*, and the nation-wide paranormal talk radio show *Coast to Coast AM*.

I have purchased a ticket to attend tonight's event, which cost me about seventy-five dollars since I tacked on the optional photo and meet-and-greet, because I want to communicate with a ghost. And The Adolphus seems like as good a place as any to facilitate that kind of communication. It's an historic building with Victorian décor—long velvet drapes framing the floor-to-ceiling windows, each tied back with a thick golden rope; ornately carved wooden furniture with fine upholstery; brass statuettes of women and horses; an oversized staircase with a wide-curling bannister, the steps lined with red carpet, like a tongue falling from a slack mouth. As I gaze around the room trying to take everything in, I can't help but think to myself, *yes*, this is very much the kind of place where I might hope to see old women holding hands in a circle, ectoplasm oozing through the knots in their hair and creeping out from beneath their petticoats.

☺

The pursuit of a continued existence beyond death is nothing new, of course. Presumably not long after we humans came to grips with our own mortal state, we started looking for ways to overcome it. The ancient Egyptians prepared tombs filled with the deceased person's belongings, sometimes including several of his or her favorite pets and servants, who were sacrificed so they could accompany their master to the land of the dead ruled by Osiris. Ancient Greeks sealed the mouths of their dead with small tokens or coins. They believed the fare was required by Charon, the ferryman, who would bear them across the river Styx into the underworld governed by Hades. Greeks also sometimes buried or burned their dead alongside chiseled tablets made of gold—now referred to by the German term

Totenpass—which detailed instructions for navigating the afterlife. And, for generations, Mexicans and their ancestors have celebrated Día De Muertos, now more commonly known as Día De Los Muertos, upon which relatives of the deceased prepare food and altars in the dead's honor, spend time socializing at their graves, and leave parting gifts in the form of their former possessions. This enduring ritual, which is believed to have originated from a pre-colonial Aztec festival, has since absorbed Spanish colonial and Christian elements and is now celebrated in many parts of the world.

The moral of these stories is that people don't want to die. And our desire not to die, combined with the coinciding knowledge that we must, is often dealt with or brought to terms by way of faith, beliefs shaped by one tradition or another that seek to reassure us there's a lot more to death than lights out. In the modern Western world, though, faith has become an increasingly rocky and crevice-filled landscape to traverse. We don't just want faith, we want *proof*. Because, after all—given the seemingly infinite scientific breakthroughs humanity has witnessed over just the last twenty or so years—we think, *shouldn't there be some kind of way to measure the dead, or to calculate them, or see them, or actually find them by now?*

☺

I have always wanted to believe in ghosts—which, I suppose, is different from actually believing in them. As a kid I played with tarot cards and Ouija boards; I asked them about all of my dead relatives, and about my favorite dogs, Corkie and Ginger. I wrote letters to the dead on my small Ninja Turtle notepad, and spoke out loud to them when I couldn't fall asleep.

Even years later, as a nearly-grown woman of eighteen, I couldn't shake the feeling that I might one day really see or talk to a dead person. That year I set out looking for my uncle, Greg, who'd recently died from a heart attack on the beach just outside our family's condo on South Padre Island. He was forty-four at the time and had three young sons, one of whom he was teaching to surf. Just a few months before his death, Uncle Greg and I had gotten tattoos together. Mine—a thick wreath of yellow roses and leafy, thorn-riddled vines encircling my thigh like a wedding garter—was a gift from him for committing to attend college and receiving a scholarship. His was a tattoo of the ocean on his foot. It looked as if his foot was completely

submerged. Frothy wavelets lapped across the
bones of his ankle, curling up towards the center
of his calf, and beneath them small, colorful
minnows circled a solid layer of blue, skirting
little tufts of sea grass lining the sole of his foot.

After Uncle Greg died, I would sit for
hours on end in our condo's living room, alone,
with the balcony door open and the sea breeze
stinging my cheeks. I would think, for a moment,
that I could see a thin coil of smoke rising from
the ashtray that once cradled his Marlboro 27s.
Then I would catch just a flicker of his red t-shirt
and jeans through the open doorway leading to
the main bedroom. More truthfully, though, I
probably just wanted to see those things so badly
that I finally did. I would stare so intently into the
empty void around me that tears would start to
well up beneath my eyes, blurring them and
mixing everything up. Fatigue distorted my sense
of shapes and colors. I was willing myself to
hallucinate, to somehow manifest Uncle Greg in
a tangible way again, and I would do it even if the
only tools I had to construct him with were the
broken off shards of my own psyche.

☉

Audrey Niffenegger once wrote, "Ghosts
can be grief gone awry."

⊙

Grief is capable of causing derangement, and evidently it has been since the dawn of living sentience. Chimpanzees grieve; so do dolphins. Elephants cry and trumpet as they circle the bones of their kin. Some dogs have even been known to lie listlessly at the foot of their master's grave, or below his or her funeral casket, or at the site of his or her death, either sure or unsure of the force that relentlessly drives them to keep watch there. And humans—well, we know what we do. At least we claim to know.

For reasons that could be traced back to any number of motivational catalysts, or could be linked to a whole combination of them—the genuine attempt to offer comfort, or jointly seek answers, or the attempt to simply capitalize, to seek profit—a subculture has now grown around the modern notion of ghosts, and around our renewed desire to prove their existence. It's worth noting, for example, that an online dating service launched in the summer of 2015 called ParanormalDate.com now boasts over 44,000 members and counting. Books tackling the subject are constantly being published, too. Some intend to explore spiritual explanations, or detail unexplained occurrences and coincidences.

Others are set on presenting a more scientific angle, one based on calculations and facts. Still more purport to bridge the gap between both approaches. Mary Roach's *Spook* (2005), Concetta Bertoldi's *Do Dead People Watch You Shower?* (2007), and Claire Bidwell Smith's *After This* (2015) make up just a few of the more recent examples.

At the same time, reality TV shows like the SyFy channel's *Ghost Hunters*, Travel Channel's *Ghost Adventures*, and Living TV's *Most Haunted* (UK) pepper the grid of both cable and satellite guide pages. The shows' hosts typically stalk the hallways of abandoned buildings—asylums, prisons, hotels—or explore participants' businesses or homes, while whispering cartoonishly and jumping at shadows. As each season progresses, they also tend to wield increasingly dubious looking devices, which claim to measure and record the presence of spirits. Commercial-grade EMF detectors (or electromagnetic field detectors), heat sensitive thermo-cameras, and old-fashioned cassette recorders now represent only the tip of the iceberg. One of the newer inventions—the REM Pod with Shadow Detection—could be described as a regular camera tripod with a coffee can

45

mounted on it, wrapped in duct tape, with a slab of Styrofoam and an antenna layered on top. And another modern marvel, the Shakti Helmet, requires the additional purchase of a cut-in-half Ping-Pong ball, which is supposed to be taped over the helmet wearer's eyes. I swear to God. Of course, the aspiring ghost hunter will also need several expensive Vortex Domes, Parascopes, and Ovilus Series Energy Whistles if he intends to maintain any measure of credibility.

☉

As I continue to wait at the Adolphus, I notice that the two women in front of me in line have struck up an especially animated conversation. They both have short, coarse grey hair and appear to be in their early-to-mid sixties. Although I overheard them introducing themselves to each other when we first settled into the waiting area several minutes ago, it seems like they're now connecting like old friends—kindred souls? At the moment they're trading stories about all of the ways their various deceased loved ones have tended to make their presence known from the "other side." Another middle-aged woman, farther ahead of us, peers her head back and chimes in.

"I wish my husband would do that," she

says wistfully, referring to a story about a spirit who was known to turn the TV off and on without warning. "That's why I'm here. I haven't heard a thing from him. And, well, I just want to make sure he's okay up there." Her voice cracks a little as she finishes her sentence, and she sort of wrinkles her nose.

The two women in front of me quickly move to reassure her. "Oh honey," one says, "I'm sure he is. And I'll bet Chip is going to let you know that tonight."

"That's right," the other woman affirms. "Chip always knows which spirits to pay closest attention to. I went to another reading of his just last year in Atlanta. He's really a wonderful blessing."

⊙

Not wanting to miss out on her own chance to see what the ghost craze was all about, my dear friend Maggie, a long-time journalist and writer, recently pitched a story to *Palm Springs Life* magazine. It required her to spend a night in the hotel room where Gram Parson's died. The magazine picked up the story, and within a few weeks Maggie found herself in room number eight of the Joshua Tree Inn. In a phone conversation we had early that evening, Maggie reiterated her assertion that she didn't really believe in ghosts, but hey, it was a free hotel room. Plus, paranormal investigations through the lens of a skeptic seemed to be all the rage at the moment.

Later that night, though, in a text message marked as delivered to me at 1:16 AM, Maggie changed her tune: "So, a cowboy hat fell off the wall and a homemade Ouija board fell out of it," she said. I asked her all the usual questions that most reasonable people would think to ask: Had she checked the room for rigging; was there anything suspicious about the wall where the hat was hanging; did she hear any mechanical noises? She said that she had checked the room earlier, and no, nothing seemed suspicious or out of place. In the final version of her article—published by *Palm Springs Life* in April of 2016 under the title "Highway 62 Revisited"—Maggie recounted the event like this:

"…I hear a noise at the foot of the bed, and I flick on the lamp. A gold cowboy hat, hung from a nail on the cinder-block wall, has fallen to the floor. The impact loosens a wooden plank about the size of a paperback. It's a homemade Ouija board. The black marker handwriting is ragged, ominous, particularly at the bottom of the board where the words "good" and "bye" are scrawled, separated by a black star. I can hardly breathe. Highway 62 unravels through the desert like a ribbon, but the road out seems so far away.

When day finally comes, the morning sky looks like a bruised knee, deep blue, mottled purple, a yellow tinge around the edges. I've slept a little, but not well.

Something else has happened during the night. Gram Parsons' music hasn't changed, but my understanding of it has. There's a difference between listening to music and hearing it, and in room No. 8, I heard."

Maggie is my friend, of course, and because I know her so well I feel inclined to believe her—she maintains that her time at the Joshua Tree Inn changed her outlook on the paranormal, and that what happened that night defies any natural explanation. But my purpose is not to coax anyone into revising their spiritual beliefs based on the account of my friend who I deem credible. Instead, I want to point out the fact that Maggie's story caused me to reconsider the other ghost stories I've heard over the years—from friends, relatives, and acquaintances—and by extension I began to consider how many of us must have heard these stories, or at some point even shared a story of our own. Could so many people really be hallucinating things or making stuff up? Surely they couldn't all be legitimately crazy. So, I found myself asking, what if there was another force at play, and what if that force was something like loss?

I suggest this connection because it seems fairly reasonable to me, but also because it helps to account for my own irreconcilable desire to believe. It might even help me figure out how to make sense of the one time in my life when I did, truly, believe.

⊙

On the night of my own paranormal experience I was staying in an old cabin, owned by a friend of my grandparents, in the Adirondacks of upstate New York. It had been several years since Uncle Greg's death. By that time I was in my early twenties. My grandparents and I spent time in this cabin every summer; it was built in the mid-nineteenth century, and since then had continued to sit on the edge of a tiny lake, Lake Hewitt. The building itself was large—

it boasted six bedrooms, five bathrooms, a large den with a hearth, and a broad porch with a porch swing facing the lake, among other spaces. The furniture and décor had remained in the style of an early twentieth century hunting cabin, and there was no internet, television, or cell phone signal. To reach the property, my grandparents and I had to drive several miles off the main road, which was a remote highway to begin with.

At night, the surrounding darkness was absolutely penetrating. It was thick, like ink in water. As the sun set, the forest would seem to loom ever taller above the slant of the roof, and the trees would encircle the house with their intricate weavings of shadows and noises. The call of loons on the misty lake struck a haunting chord between laughter and hysteria. Even as a young woman in my twenties, I still felt a quick plunge in my stomach when I turned out the light in my room each night. I couldn't shake the distinct feeling that someone could be holding a hand inches away from my face, and in the darkness I wouldn't even see a shadow. The feeling of remoteness and isolation was so acute it felt like I was lying in a solitary, pressurized room at the bottom of the ocean floor.

During this particular summer, only my

grandmother and I had come to the lake. We were staying in separate bedrooms on the second floor of the house, and our rooms were connected by a shared bathroom. The only other occupant in the house at the time was my grandparents' friend, a man I called Uncle Gus, who had inherited the property from his mother.

One night, about midway through our trip, my grandmother and I both retired to our rooms around the same time. For a while, as I lay in bed reading, I could hear her washing her face in the bathroom between us, the door to which was slightly ajar. But, by the time I turned off the lamp beside me, I could tell she had gone to bed too. All was quiet and the bathroom was dark. As I lay there trying to fall asleep, I felt unusually bothered by the empty silence. The air around me felt more dense than usual. So, although I had never done so before in that house, I began to talk out loud to Uncle Greg. I asked him to stay near me and protect me. I said, *Please don't show up or make noises or anything—you'll scare me. Just be here. Please tell all the other ghosts to go away. Please keep me safe.*

In the morning, when I came downstairs to join my grandmother for breakfast, she said, "Why did you put the toilet seat up in our bathroom? I had to go in the middle of the night and I nearly fell in!" I told her I hadn't used the restroom since before she'd gotten ready for bed the night before. I hadn't even walked through it. "No," she said, "that's impossible. Because when I got ready for bed, the toilet seat was down." She reminded me that Uncle Gus had his own bathroom, and that he had trouble climbing the stairs—and anyway, why would he walk through one of our bedrooms to use the restroom in the middle of the night? She laughed, almost nervously. "I mean, who else could it have been? I'm telling you, I almost fell in!"

It was true that, aside from the three of us, no one else had been in the house. But I knew that I had not put the toilet seat up in the middle of the night. Why would I? I'd never put a toilet seat up in my life, except to clean the one in my own home. Uncle Greg was a prankster, though. I couldn't help but remember how, back in middle school, he used to take my friends and me to toilet paper the yards of boys we had crushes on in school. And I'd also heard that, back when he was just a kid himself, he'd been known to tear through the halls of a nursing home owned by his grandmother—my great-grandmother— wearing nothing but a cape made out of an old sheet. As far as I was concerned, the toilet seat served as unequivocal proof that Uncle Greg had heard me the night before. He'd done exactly what I asked; he didn't manifest himself or make a noise—but he wanted me to know he was there. Knowing the way he'd always horsed around in life, I figured he'd probably hoped I would be the one to almost fall in the toilet. A little jab of the elbow to the ribs.

☉

Is there such thing as a crossing point between desire and truth? Can we want something so badly it becomes real?

☉

Back at the Adolphus, hotel staff members have finally opened up the doors to small parlor where Chip will be speaking and performing a group reading, and we're beginning to make our way inside. I count twenty rows of chairs in the room. As each person files in behind me, I watch them examine the chairs, too. We're all assessing our chance of being noticed, and therefore of being singled out for a reading. *Maybe he'll purposely choose someone from the back,* someone's thinking. Or, *If I sit here in the third row I won't seem too eager, but I'll still have a window to be seen.* I sit in the third row, hoping to be chosen.

When Chip finally enters the room, the hushed swell of anticipation becomes tangible. He introduces himself, spends about an hour presenting a brief lecture on his experiences as a paranormal investigator, and then says it's time for the psychic reading to begin. We are told that if we want to be considered for a reading, we should silently raise one hand—not all the way up, he cautions, just as high as our faces—and wait for him to call on someone. Chip explains that he'll attempt to communicate with the deceased loved ones of the person he has called on, then he'll begin the process of choosing a new subject again.

Each time our hands go up, I notice they go a little higher. Some people are flicking them back and forth a little; some are smiling or raising their eyebrows, straining to make eye contact. Other people, like me, are attempting to appear nonchalant. I sometimes glance down at my lap, pretending to pick a small piece of lint off my pants with the hand that's not raised. Then I slowly scan the room, making a conscious effort to look at anyone besides Chip.

Each time Chip begins the selection process again, every person's hand goes up. We all want a chance to hear from the people or person we've lost. It's written all over our faces, including my own face I'm sure. We crane our necks to be seen, to have our pain acknowledged, and the grief we brought with us hovers above our heads, like a white balloon tied to the wrist of each raised hand. Looking into the faces of everyone around me—a man silently crying, holding a baseball cap to his chest, or a woman, anxious and exhausted, wiggling her fingertips in the air like a school girl—I can't help but feel like I'm staring into my own face, my own fears. Death suddenly becomes so palpable I can see it flickering in front of me, like a limpid, reflective mirage. I can reach out and touch it.

Moments later, though, I notice the reading is about to come to an end. Chip still hasn't called on me, and I realize that I'm not going to hear from Uncle Greg. Many other women won't get to hear from their aunts or uncles, either. Or from their children, who might have made it to five, or fourteen, or thirty. Many husbands won't hear from their wives, or speak to their brothers.

At one point, just before calling it a night, I could have sworn that Chip looked right at me. He paused for a moment, thought about whether to read me, but then he shifted his gaze across the room.

Or maybe he never paused at all. Maybe I only wanted to believe that—in the same way I wanted to believe that the room we were in was full of dead people, and that they were clamoring to be seen and heard just as we were straining to see and hear them. There are so many things I want to believe. I remember how, early on in the program, Chip told the woman who'd lost her husband that he wanted her to start turning the lights off when she slept. I remember wanting to believe that the message had really come from beyond, and that the woman would now be able to turn the lights off, and that she'd find a way to survive in that darkness. I don't know whether I believe in ghosts or not, but I know that when I sleep with the lights on, it's not because I'm afraid of something lurking in the shadows; it's because I'm afraid there might not be anything there at all.

Afterword

Years ago, when I was an undergraduate studying poetry in Jenny Browne's class at Trinity University, she wrote a very unusual word on the board: "lighght." You may recognize this word as Aram Saroyan's famous visual poem, which sparked intense controversy and nearly led to the complete destruction of the National Endowment for the Arts after the NEA paid for the piece to be included in their 1969 issue of *The American Literary Anthology*.

I didn't know anything about the poem's history at the time, but I knew that it thrilled me. The word opened up just enough to spill out its own light, to *become* light, or a kind of lightness. Rather than the arbitrary distance that typically exists between signifiers and their concepts, the two things seemed to suddenly join together; there was a hidden truth, a hidden reality, inside this word "lighght."

What I'm saying is: the poem manifested light. It made something out of nothing. It didn't just refer to an object beyond itself (beyond language?), but actually appeared to turn into that thing, like a magic trick.

Have you ever woken up in the middle of the night and felt your skin prickling at the base of your skull—felt like somewhere, inside the blackness above you, an unknown presence was hovering—a power? A fear?

All my life these kinds of entities have floated near me. Maybe they're deep-set primal instincts emerging from my psyche, or weighty associations, or even gaslit old memories: the glimmering eyes I was told not to speak of, to pretend I'd never seen. And all my life, I've wished that I could reach into my own darkness and touch those hovering beings—like the skin of shadow, or the flesh of grief. What if I could turn on the light and look into their real faces, without them shrinking away? What if I could show everyone?

In 2007, when Aram Saroyan spoke with Ian Daily about his poem "lighght," he said: "the crux of the poem is to try and make the ineffable, which is light—which we only know about because it illuminates something else—into a *thing*."

Like many poets, I realize our world is rarely simple or neat. "Objective" reality—to the extent that it exists—is messy, layered, and flaky. And so I've tried to create a kind of lenticular quality within my "minml" poems. In other words, if you view them from one angle, you might see one thing, but then if you shift to a different angle, you might see something else.

This is my inquiry: If I could cast enough light (or "lighght," perhaps?) to show you every entity that has haunted, or pestered, or even sometimes delighted me—the one that resembles a tiny, flat conflation between *woman* and *womb*, for example; or the one gargoyling itself between *female* and *femme* and *pheromone*; or this one mangling *garbage* and *baggage* and *garb* into a solitary, loopy pile—what would those look like to you?

In the poem "White Mountain," Vievee Francis writes, "I walk around the property thinking I might happen upon / the source of the sound. How could that cry be wind alone?" She says, "It seems / as if I might ride the beast that haunts me if I could just let go."

I guess there are things I've been trying to let go of—but it's hard to let go of the empty space inside a picture frame, or a puddle of smoke. It's hard to let go when you've never quite been able to hold on in the first place. So, what if I gave my ghosts their own substance and breath; would I finally be able to tuck them in and let them sleep? Could I shut the door and walk away?

Gratitude

This little book owes so much to so many wonderful writers, friends, and relatives, but for now I will try to keep things "minml." I want to thank my family—especially my mom and dad, brothers and sisters, and Grammy—for always having my back, even when I invest my time in projects as unusual as this one. I love you guys. I also would not have been able to write these pieces—or anything, actually—without the support of my mentors at Trinity University, The University of California at Riverside, and Texas Tech University. Thank you all for caring about and teaching me. I'm so grateful to have had the support of Cooper Dillon Books in bringing this project to life, too; it's been a lucky experience, in particular, to benefit from the editorial insight of Adam Deutsch. Finally, my work both here and elsewhere is most indebted to the few writers who I'm lucky enough to call friends. In particular, I want to thank Maggie Downs for knowing to text me every time she encounters a ghost, Chloe Honum for encouraging me to send this chapbook out, and Chen Chen for spending too many hours on Skype deconstructing the nuances of using one 'f' or two in some of these little poems. You people are the heart of my heart.

Mag Gabbert holds a PhD in creative writing from Texas Tech University and an MFA from The University of California at Riverside. Her essays and poems have been published in *32 Poems, Waxwing, The Rumpus, Thrush, The Cortland Review, Phoebe, Birmingham Poetry Review,* and many other journals. Mag teaches creative writing at Southern Methodist University and for Writing Workshops Dallas. She serves as the interviews editor for *Underblong Journal.*